ACCUSATION TO RUIN

KAREN KELLOCK PH.D.

Manual for
Superior Men

A complete theory based on Einstein physics,
Political Psychology, Systems Theory
and Archetypal Psychiatry.

FORMULA
All success attraction
All disease obstruction
All recovery elimination

You must fast on all three
OBSTRUCTIONS:
People
Habit
Food

ACCUSATION TO RUIN

How she fights socially is most cruel. Suddenly you're deposed, fired or flunk school.   You know she's discussing you with others [disgraced] judging from frowns on their faces.   It's a morally degraded society when females take control over thee. The Jezebel mothers became loudmouthed cranks addicted to power or they drank. Because Jezebel is out of grace, she messes up big time and now its your problem.

ACCUSATION
TO RUIN

SHREWD UNDERHANDED COMPARISONS
WE SWIM IN MUDDY WATERS
SUPERFICIALITY AND SHALLOWNESS
HUMILIATING COMPETITIONS
TALLY THE WAYS THEY HURT
INVASION OF COARSENESS
MASTURBATION: FIZZLING OUT
A BROKEN SPIRIT WANTS EVERYTHING
FEMALE COMPETITION BLOCKS SUPPORT
STATIONARY COMPLAINTS
EVER LEARNING BUT NEVER WIZENED
WHY COMPLAIN WHAT YOU CAN CHANGE
A BROKEN VESSEL IS ALWAYS COMPARING
EVIL SPIRIT OF COMPROMISE
DANGEROUS MEN ARE TEACHERS
TOO WEAK TO SAY "BE GONE"
SETTLING FOR LESS
CREEPY, FLAKY AND SELFISH
LOOKING BACK IS LOW, HARD
SELFIE: LAZY AND SLEAZY
PLASTIC SURGEONS REIGN
TACTICAL COMPARISONS
HEAL: STOP TALKING
ADDICTION TO BUMS
WORDS USED AS GUNS
PEOPLE IN THEIR SYSTEMS
IT'S NOT DOMINATION IT'S TRUST
THE DURESS OF EARLY YEARS
PNEUMATICITY: MAKE A SPACE
SMEAR CAMPAIGNS SEEN LATER
WE'RE NOT MADE FOR RELATIONSHIP
INSECURITY TRASHES COLLABORATIONS
BROKEN & FEELING WORTHLESS

ACCUSATION TO RUIN

BROKEN QUEENS DEVALUED
TRIGGERING FALSE COMPARISONS
SECURITY & CONFIDENCE AREN'T LOUD
SUCCESS AFTER SEASON OF TREASON
INSECURITY AND SHAME
THE WORLD TRASHES SELF
ROYAL COUPLE OBSTRUCTIONS
RUIN FROM NO SELF-CONFIDENCE
COMING TO YOUR APEX
INTERLOCKING JEALOUSY PATTERNS
GROUPTHINK AND MOB RULE
TARGETS GET NERVOUS IN PUBLIC
THE NARCISSIST IS SO BORIN
SINNERS LOSE THEIR GUILTY STAIN
SIN BRINGS GHASTLY UGLINESS
WHEN HE SWITCHED TO A MADMAN
HOW TRAUMA BLOCKS SUCCESS
FEAR OF SUCCESS: PATHOLOGICAL ENVY
DON'T GIVE EM A CHANCE
FRENEMY ABUSE
STOP RUNNING YOUR MOUTH
NEVER CHASE A MAN
THE PRICE OF EXPOSURE
ARCHETYPAL PSYCHIATRY RULES
THE END IS THE APEX OF LIFE
TO GO GLOBAL, BE CONSERVATIVE
FEMALE TREACHERY
NO COMPETITION WITH GOD
PATHOLOGICAL ENVY: FATHERS/SONS
DEEP THOUGHT PEOPLE
BASHED FOR HAVING NO FRIEND
OVERCOMING BAD IDENTITY
JEZEBEL MOTHERS ARE LOUDMOUTH CRANKS
JEZEBEL FIGHTS WITH SOCIAL TACTICS

ACCUSATION
TO RUIN

ACCUSATION
TO RUIN

ACCUSATION
TO RUIN

My work is my destiny and it's all talkin psychology cuz I went quite mad in a sick system hell see.

Family treacheries are basis of Greek tragedy--that's how basic it is but Christ brought a sword see.

Mental and emotional torture is surely not as bad as physical but it is excruciating and a fall.

An incredible rare talent yet with self-esteem problems like the rest of us. It's now in our DNA sis.

SHREWD UNDERHANDED COMPARISONS

The minute I got into town she looked me up and down then targeted my sorry self from then on.

His shrewd underhanded comparisons makes her wake up weak, question herself, energy down.

Comparisons destroy self-esteem because there ARE no comparisons with a real queen see.

Comparisons disrupt feminine dignity. Suddenly she's in the backseat and he doesn't care see.

ACCUSATION TO RUIN

It's. a **STING** when comparisons disrupt feminine dignity and create desperation in her soul see.

Comparisons poison the sisterhood with divide-and-conquer strivings and that means treachery.

"You called me a pig, you left me off in other cities, you said I was yappy, go to hell creepy." -Lady

You said you would do it but did nothing at all. You made promises then disappeared into hell.

Shrewd comparisons to relatives, siblings, neighbors and at a certain point to the *younger*.

Wicked comparisons then boob/nose jobs or any other device changing how you're made by God.

You can be so happy as a carefree child then you wake up terrified in comparison culture, aye.

That old black cloud God has made white & pure as snow and buried it--He hath forgotten it all.

These are tactical comparisons: they know what they're doing with shit-shots causing desperation.

WE SWIM IN MUDDY WATERS

Since we swim in muddy waters we assume it's better tho' it's contaminated, poison, a wrecker.

Why do they hate you? Cuz you're not a clone and could never be---they can't bring you down.

You weren't bad just caught up in the muck with a chump--it happens when they load you up.

How many great geniuses have died too early having been ganged up on by tribe or family?

ACCUSATION TO RUIN

WAR is the ontologically fatal insight that the world is not what you thought it was: BLIGHT.

Comparisons are based on superficial traits generating desires in one that are never fulfilled ok.

It used to be we wanted to be thin, now we're all conforming to heavier-- curvaceous is in.

SUPERFICIALITY AND SHALLOWNESS

Superficiality, shallowness, meanness at novelty: this keeps our reality bland, sad, unfree.

As envy sets in she has doctor shoot up her derriere like a hippo for that butt in those she knows.

She has doctors shoot stuff in her lips to bloat up like a bubble out of conformity to you all.

Every cell has a memory and I felt [feel] trauma in every cell and that's a description of PTSD hell.

A cell memory of what it felt like in that system and the secret realignments against That One.

Relocate and now you're just a name. More like a legend depending how much you sinned ok.

Her frame couldn't carry such big boobs a doctor put on her chest but all the comparisons did that.

Looks, size: comparison compensations are a never ending cycle and one is never satisfied.

HUMILIATING COMPETITIONS

Then she gets in humiliating competitions with other women, blocking her from helping them.

ACCUSATION TO RUIN

You developed an art form/wrote a book. Now you're saved from ageist remarks by chumps.

The most famous writers in history were rejected early. It was the fuel in their tank to work constantly.

Identity is relational. Who you are defines who they are. Why they hate: if you're a success they're losers.

Half is your talent and work and the other half is overcoming the jerks--more like two thirds.

They are violent but don't forget they're kids with brittle emotions--handle shrewdly for safety.

So what do we have so far: mean comparisons, petty competitions and groupthink backstabbins'.

TALLY THE WAYS THEY HURT

Tally the ways people keep you down, make you frown & ruin the day when you coulda been glowin'.

You're a world famous salsa jazz musician and what do they have: weddings, funerals and CNN.

I suffer from something called not enough time. I'd love to know you better but destiny's here, aye.

It happened. You screwed up. You got weak and the devil had a field day: repent and go on.

Sorry you haven't heard from me but I was still sore after conversating with a commie lady.

It wasn't you but the underbelly of the collective unconscious erupting from weakness.

Bible gives room to meat-eaters & meat-abstainers. Living on fruit, leaves & cheese is not inferior.

ACCUSATION TO RUIN

Stop comparing me to others for there is no bigger insult brother cuz God's in me and uniquely clever.

Both pathological envy and excruciating shame are inherited thru the system so stop it ok?

INVASION OF COARSENESS

A coarseness of vulgarity and cruelty has taken over the culture and you need a locked gate for sure.

In this culture you were likely mentally ill at previous levels but no worry we all were/it's the devil.

We have a 1st amendment in this country. I don't wanna argue with you & I'll say what I want honey.

When you finally put God before people you see the first page of Psalms is true: they're out to get you.

When women compete with each other they open a door for unscrupulous characters taking over.

Every kingdom, city or house divided against itself comes to desolation and shall not stand.

With sister competition she no longer understands her true value and she's no longer a queen too.

Was it mental illness, immaturity, addiction or sin? It was all of them, basically synonymous son.

Modernity say it's all good but they're dead wrong. We've a generation of zombies/a dense throng.

How we're devil cursed: it all works at first then it all turns on the victim of dangerous myths.

The carnivore diet works at first but with many soon you see eye-bags, a sign of kidney blockages.

ACCUSATION TO RUIN

If I ate a steak I'd have eyebags hanging down to my waist. A hypersensitive no longer ace.

The devil works at first, and he waits. The sober alki who resumes drinking glows, then goes low.

The things we're most allergic to work at first then are a curse but we just can't forget that first.

MASTURBATION: FIZZLING OUT

Masturbation is both cause & symptom of insanity cuz It tracks the mind into hellish fantasy.

Masturbation is a symptom of insanity. Devoid of good reason/goals its all animal instincts see.

They insist on being called gay not homosexual--maybe cuz inside they know it's wrong ya know?

Masturbation creates feeblemindedness so don't listen to your teachers in kindergarten no less.

Masturbation is both cause and result of insanity and we hear about it so much these days.

The saints have a conscience and suffer remorse more than most. The others couldn't care less.

We're not meant to fizzle out but succumb quickly to onset of age-related conditions: high then die.

A BROKEN SPIRIT WANTS EVERYTHING

With a broken spirit you want everything but what God uniquely gave you and never satisfied too.

When women war like this against each other they open the door to unscrupulous characters.

ACCUSATION TO RUIN

This third nostril has a field day in all their lives. He's now the go-between hearing their cries.

Two women cursing each other, even coming to blows, over a man in the middle/king on the hill.

Women fighting on phone or in pubic over a man who didn't even deserve a conversation with em.

It started with a broken spirit that lost the concept of being a queen since others are degrading.

Emotional abuse has put her back in the position of proving herself good enough or chasing.

She no longers understands her true value at all. She has made man a god and continues to fall.

FEMALE COMPETITION BLOCKS SUPPORT

Warring against each other rather than the devil in the middle and the little man making it all go.

Compete with sisters, wreck your own support system. It's that old devil in the middle, get HIM.

If your friend takes your man he was never yours, they weren't your friends and did you a favor.

The bad guy separates her from female pillars and puts her on an island of abuse alone with him.

He separates her from female pillars putting her on an island of emotional abuse and torture.

Every time she gets a guy she alienates all the other women and could never be a good friend.

Comparisons, competition and alienation from other women: now she sees aunt as obstruction.

ACCUSATION TO RUIN

Brutal female competition making life hellish is due to broken consciousness, it's not innate.

Don't just fall in love with a man. You don't know what's IN him--it takes time and trusting God's plan.

STATIONARY COMPLAINTS

The third step of brokenness is endless complaints. You're older/options over and he's the same.

She sees how everything's gone wrong but there's no will to move forward: she's locked downward.

All her friends know she complains about it but never demonstrates a WILL to move out of it.

The more she complains the more tangled the web becomes as triangles begin to form.

The woman's complaints are the cry of a broken soul. That's the process and it means getting old.

She's complaining but never moving or changing. Any rejection locks her into codependency.

EVER LEARNING BUT NEVER WIZENED

Constantly learning lessons but always failing the test. Reading useless books and diverse lusts.

Shifting her life into a new dimension? She won't even conversate about that, she's locked in.

The spirit of codependency shifts the focus from God to man. It makes a god out of man: deception.

But this fear of man brings a snare. No man's worthy of fear, seek only God and cast your care.

ACCUSATION TO RUIN

A toxic dysfunctional norm is all she knows so despite complaining constantly that's home.

Obsessed with seeking a man's favor makes you a dam beggar. Seek only God, He's your lifesaver.

The whole time this guy was creating a demonic soul tie where you hate the lies but fear leaving, aye.

Being stuck is called Stationary Complaints. Conversation becomes pure repeat and hate.

The soul is incapacitated cuz it's incarcerated: a silenced peon can't make a sound decision.

WHY COMPLAIN WHAT YOU CAN CHANGE

Why complain about something you can change? But that's what it is as her friends disengage.

We don't wanna hear any more of her complaints. She's gotta fly away and save herself from hate.

If she were to just repent and go in the opposite direction she'd feel the power once again.

One constantly complaining is not planning to move. A wise man seeks counsel but keeps quiet too.

Educated and lettered she says "I deserve better than this" but twenty years later there she sits.

Choose your pain: the pain of life wasted or pain leaving a dude who doesn't deserve you anyway.

A BROKEN VESSEL IS ALWAYS COMPARING

A broken queen compares herself to everybody, not ever content with what God gave her see.

ACCUSATION TO RUIN

The next move on the highway of lost queens is the humiliating competition with other ladies.

She's even competing against her best friend. Here there develops jealousy triangles and ruin.

The last point is a total and complete compromise: giving into opinions around her until she dies.

Rating women 1-10: "I'm in my fifties, i'm a TWO", How pathetic looking at yourself this way Sue.

No one has a right to rate me. Beauty is subjective/in the eye of the beholder so it's arrogant see.

Most women have never heard that voice saying the unimaginable thing: "you are a queen".

EVIL SPIRIT OF COMPROMISE

What does a woman do who doesn't know that? Compromise: sink in her swill and give up.

I had a broken spirit and it took a toll on my total psyche. Nothing worked, hate and lunacy.

With a broken spirit with everything I saw I feared it. My soul was sick, I said stupid things like "shit".

The break was traumatic then a spiraling down with increasingly dangerous people around.

All the while being in total denial about what's going on, saving me from psychotic shock full-blown.

DANGEROUS MEN ARE TEACHERS

What took me to the brink was a dangerous man in his 20's pestering me until I gave in/let him in.

ACCUSATION TO RUIN

I had never experienced such psychopathy, sadism, lack of empathy and self-serving narcissism.

He invited his friends and they robbed me too--in a human zoo I had alcoholically mal-adapted to.

I never knew people like this existed and it taught me more than a library of books on the kids.

Others were the same: time-wasting, encroaching, imposing, manipulative and all self-serving.

TOO WEAK TO SAY "BE GONE"

These losers were high school '85 so I can imagine what it's like now in blue states advancing lies.

The fear and trauma from this mobbing experience encrypted my identity for permanence.

It's an entirely social generation as taught in the schools. Man before God, worshipping fools.

If you weren't social they might attack, taking it personally you're rejecting them in fact.

I was too weak, hypnotized and timid to say "I just want to be alone, please leave" so became prey.

If you're too weak to say "I want to be alone"--those five little words--you've lost your lovely home.

Why would a queen commingle with fools or even participate in a discussion without rules?

She speaks from a podium or not at all because she knows they'll likely target her kind for a fall.

SETTLING FOR LESS

ACCUSATION TO RUIN

So sad when she didn't have strength to try anymore. "That's who I am, just a two and his whore."

"I'll never be worth any more than this. I'm just gonna settle, count my blessings and not resist."

A lady at seventy has attractive energy if she hasn't allowed the world to break the queen see.

A woman at fifty says she's "done" and is lackluster in spirit because she hasn't truly overcome.

A lady at seventy can be mesmerizing if she hasn't allowed the world to break her focusing.

Many at fifty still have the Jezebel spirit: catty, gossipy, invoking groupthink to chime in with.

Where does this spirit of compromise come from? Broken consciousness: the devil won.

She wants a relationship so bad she compromises. It's so wrong yet the world applauds it sis.

I pray every soul tie, toxic connection and spirit of compromise are now canceled in Jesus name.

CREEPY, FLAKY AND SELFISH

Creepy, flaky and out only for themselves. They hang with like kind and impose on you unawares.

Shut up buddy: comparisons wreck self-esteem and female dignity but you know that already.

Sister stop saying you care about women. You care only if they conform to your way of thinkin'.

Comparisons are shrewd and underhanded, coming at just the right moment: social demons.

ACCUSATION TO RUIN

You used me till I was all used up but at least you got your money [furniture, etc] and I'm all-ok.

You used me the mentally ill but at least you got the sex you craved with a scared empty vessel.

You [who I despise] used me [emotionally traumatized] but at least you can brag to all the guys.

LOOKING BACK IS LOW, HARD

Looking back I can't believe it but that's how it goes. Thats why memories are anchors to go low.

Is there a woman existing who hasn't been molested by age ten? Religious cults, but its by friends.

The whole culture didn't just slide to the left it slid into hell: perverted expectations of many/y'all.

Sitting in a family gathering and suddenly Uncle Joe's talking about Deep Throat: falling to lows.

Off-color jokes [not even sexual or bathroom humor] is how it starts in homes. Be rigid or alone.

The whole culture slid into hell in the seventies and off-color inanities have taken center stage see.

"Perform" oral sex or you're a social reject, not part of the liberal elect, not with it man: SICK!

Get down on your knees and degrade yourself see--this is a sickening scene for a queen, ya think?

It's a severe undertow taking over and thus there are no queens just make-believe fem cheerleaders.

Even with lesbians escaping male comparisons they start up soon to maintain homeostasis.

ACCUSATION TO RUIN

SELFIE: LAZY AND SLEAZY

These perverted expectations started with the kids [brainwashed twits] so now don't you do it.

I was terrified when they accused me of things they had heard about and filthy minds shout out.

It's hard to get the dirty images outa your mind in a culture that's constantly saying it's fine.

All that pain you put me thru gave me a new life of writing about people like you. Thank you.

Emotionally traumatized her skin hung in folds but when happy again it snapped back/not old.

Both male and female culture are geared to reject novelty so the life of smart is very rocky.

Just like your siblings, when you went off to liberal college I changed my opinion of you see.

You are now someone I don't wanna know. We live in opposite universes so goodbye you liberal.

Now I'm on top you're coming around in prayer but I recall how you backstabbed to the lawyer.

PLASTIC SURGEONS REIGN

Everyone wants to be someone or something they are not. Very few are content made by God.

She compares herself to you and you to her but neither considers yourselves valuable: bummer.

Suddenly you both feel you're not enough. And when that happens identity degrades to fluff.

ACCUSATION TO RUIN

Your identity moved from a high class store to a walmart shelf by these comparisons from hell.

Constant comparisons makes em behave like fools. Temporal, fleeting things: looks, size, cute.

Comparing breaks the foundations of a woman's self-esteem and dignity--it's below us really.

TACTICAL COMPARISONS

He slides into your life [lovebombing woo] then injects comparisons to female opposites of you.

He's throwing this stuff out to work on her soul subliminally but queens never allow this buddy.

He's constantly comparing with other women while your fragile self-esteem is hopelessly degradin'.

Would a king sit in her presence if she said how fine this man is/how handsome that one--serious?

Most importantly beloved, don't trash new relationships with sad stories of past ones--how foolish.

She's always bringing the past present so a new guy has to counsel her out of it then substitute.

HEAL: STOP TALKING

Heal then stop talking sad stories or reserve em for meetings or a book but for love get a grip.

It's the same pattern: the new guy acts as a counselor to heal her emotions then she loves him.

The enemy wants to bring you down into memory or the old identity so keep saying: you're FREE.

ACCUSATION TO RUIN

The best saints WERE the worst sinners in enontiodromia: converting into the opposite.

Guilt, shame and embarrassment. Guilt, shame and embarrassment. It's no way to live God said.

Trauma hits: all the energy comes inside a person to self-defend and the result is a narcissist.

Liberty necessitates virtue. You won't have freedom to sin or someone will come in to remove it.

The elites at the top are mean petulant children out for self while totally and ruthlessly ruling us.

They can't take one tenth what they dish out. They're cruel and they're haughty put-downs loud.

When he wants to degrade her self-esteem & dignity he slides female images in to create jealousy.

It's a helluva thing when siblings get their attorneys in on the scapegoat game then it sticks ok.

They are so dam dominant and they're mean about it. I couldn't stand it for one minute, I'd get out.

The new life will be wonderful, the extreme opposite to the old one which was miserable.

ADDICTION TO BUMS

Addiction to bums: YES, I said it, you've fallen way below all that that God has ordained in sum.

When insecurity takes over they overestimate others they see and underestimate the self see.

When they saw the giants they were in their own sight grasshoppers and assumed that of others.

ACCUSATION TO RUIN

When the toxic one sees how you view them they begin to play that role and you're screwed then.

The minute the toxic shrewd one sees you cowering they move in and take advantage darling.

When I underestimated myself in insecurity the Lord said He had a great plan and don't put it down.

The Lord said He knew me in the womb and put words in my mouth so NO one can stop me now.

It's all based on your low self-esteem so please show this bum the door when he threatens to leave.

Don't you dare underestimate yourself and overestimate a hobo or bum you've taken in. Yuk ma'am.

Having underestimated myself I let the overestimated bum in and he took over way back then.

WORDS USED AS GUNS

The things you said about me to other people. Words have power Jane, you incited riots so evil.

The way people treated me after talking to you. A clear give away but I was so in denial, who knew.

It's the Way People Treated Me After Talking To You. Yes Jane, that's your gun/common to women.

And YOU ALL were her flying monkeys, going along with this smear campaign and the treacheries.

After going thru all those games you're likely angry. Don't transfer this to others now sweety.

Your faux paus and sins are garish in memory to you but faded replicas in others, hope this helps.

ACCUSATION TO RUIN

Your sins are glaring sirens to you but to others tucked away somehow or laughed off, so relax.

PEOPLE IN THEIR SYSTEMS

Now that you're well, the fact that you went so low is of interest and can only become profitable.

With instability it was always the same: I'd over-estimate you and under-estimate me ok.

Since genius is groundbreaking of course normies would object to it, wanting only zones of comfort.

When ridding bothersome introjects it helps to see em not as people but as actors or archetypes.

It wasn't Mary or Johnny but that archetype at that time in reaction to whatever you were doing, aye.

You'll soon be dead, they'll soon be dead, so concentrate on resolving archetypes instead.

My behavior triggered the bully archetype in her and the rest is history in decades of treachery.

We are not created for relationship but to do the Lord's work and we unite together if it all fits.

IT'S NOT DOMINATION IT'S TRUST

It's not that I dominate him it's just that he trusts my creativity cuz he knows it prospers him.

Open marriage is serial adultery. It's not the same as religious polygamy it's just plain dirty.

It's like a little nugget, a bubble or a pearl coming thru: these proverbs, 70,000 of em for you.

ACCUSATION TO RUIN

I don't dominate him he just trusts my creativity. There's a big difference & it's profitable see.

They were just little archetypes or tests to keep you down or prove you've grown, forget it now.

The clown you were with simply showed the level to which you'd fallen as an lil' addicted twit.

THE DURESS OF EARLY YEARS

Isn't it thrilling now it's all over: decades of dung working out lower archetypes with clowns.

I wrote it while going mad to understand the nature of madness from other people's influences.

I moved to desert to enjoy sun, sand, stars at night inspiring prolific write-- blocked by people blight.

Immediately the herd swooped in on me and I went into dead denial because I had no boundaries.

Boundaries: make room for a king ladies. Don't let in anyone who comes by, be selective see.

It's called pneumaticity: make a space and it fills in with the new [appropriate] immediately.

PNEUMATICITY: MAKE A SPACE

Replace thoughts of past introjects bothering you so much with future prospects, even love.

Now just live your new abundant life solo not thinking of anyone you've known when so low.

Don't underestimate yourself vis-a-vis a haughty fool cuz then you're trashing the God in you.

ACCUSATION TO RUIN

From overestimating those people to going wherever God sends you and no one can stop you.

Woman and man equals home. Woman minus man is a helluva life alone = the world's full of crones.

SMEAR CAMPAIGNS SEEN LATER

You usually don't find out or wake up to it until years later when the pieces come together.

When all the pieces come together you finally see it: it's so obvious by then you can't deny it.

How to get to success: Whatever you do, do it only to please the inner self. It decides, it selects.

They are dreamers of the human condition. Remove everything then start again: we're all lovin'?

Destroy the evil nation completely then all that's left is nice humans loving each other so sweetly.

So it all comes down to the left's view of human nature as GOOD rather than evil, bad, immature.

The scariest part of their idealism: they only consider the criminal and they disregard the victim.

They've got it all the way around and they never learn. They go right back to lovin' after being hurt.

Give up wokism and teach our kids HISTORY: that human nature doesn't ever change see.

Biden's Governing Policy: Whatever is rational, logical, helpful and protective- -do the opposite see.

The youth don't know you and your foes are dead or senile. Enjoy the rest and ignore the snide.

ACCUSATION TO RUIN

WE'RE NOT MADE FOR RELATIONSHIP

You poor kid. They bullied, used and walked right over you and you overcame and made it too.

Borrego was like being in a prison. An open society where everyone knows your business.

Hate to tell you this but we're not made for relationship. It's God, our destiny then a mate if it fits.

I'm never gonna be in that natural process where I overestimate you/underestimate again sis.

Leave toxic women alone and they will cannibalize each other from insecurities--watch em brother.

Insecurity wrecks all collaboration. It doesn't matter how brilliant one is the effect is destruction.

When she needs to collab to get to the next level she feels anxious and jealous of other women.

INSECURITY TRASHES COLLABORATIONS

Lacking security or vital self-confidence one always sabotages important partnerships.

A new sister comes in who is chic and smart and rather than gaining from her they undermine her.

Insecurities always make us small. She's trying to help you but you're thinking she wants your man.

Insecurity destroying collaborations with powerful others must be overcome to go further.

God sends us someone at a higher level to bring us up but we won't benefit if envy stops us up.

ACCUSATION TO RUIN

God wants women to work together but there's always unnecessary drama then it's all over.

Tho' it's hardest: You uproot the original trauma [missing father or cheating lover] by forgiving it.

With forgiveness she begins to release all anchors from her soul, those hurts impossible to console.

A queen washes her brain of all negativity. She replaces all that trash with truth and treasure see.

BROKEN & FEELING WORTHLESS

A woman so broken by trauma or society she's unable to plug into her own worth anymore: a tragedy.

A traumatized woman is divorced from her essence--a moving zombie disconnected and senseless.

When you look at society and women today, how many seem broken? Look at that one there--twerkin'.

A woman so disconnected is used by a generation of men so perverted they're good with it.

The wounded queen is nothing but a sex object but so broken she will find pleasure/glory in that.

Any woman with broken consciousness will be used by men for their own gain then go more insane.

The trap of broken consciousness, what does it look like? She's being humiliated and finds joy in it.

She doesn't just wake up to being used, the steps are progressive into horrors of degradation too.

BROKEN QUEENS DEVALUED

ACCUSATION TO RUIN

Toxic masculinity works thru indoctrination defining the markers of value, femininity, attraction.

The narcissistic man wants to subjugate the true queen inside--breaking her down via COMPARISONS.

The broken queen in a toxic culture becomes consumed with comparisons to other women.

She thought siblings were her friends but they weren't and she would never, ever trust em again.

Once she released those people she could finally process the years of abuse and pain too.

She said she was a Christian so I expected her to be the light and have compassion but NO MA'AM.

Socially hypnotized, accepting whatever told, never investigating further, hating novelty/creativity.

The world breaks us down by triggering comparisons--then we look down on self and up to them.

TRIGGERING FALSE COMPARISONS

That's how society thugs & princesses get to us: always by triggering comparisons so watch this.

False religions worship people, family and the social. But Christ brought a sword dividing people.

Mixed signals, sneaky put-downs, polite cruelties, aggravating comparisons, insulting questions.

Due to media they're no longer busy with individuality but are rather consumed by comparisons.

She bought into what a boss chick looks like so has now lost the sense of her own greatness/style.

ACCUSATION TO RUIN

So the first stop in the broken consciousness interstate is to put your mind only on comparisons ok.

From a happy colorful cornucopia to a grey, watered down and dizzy depression and blank slate.

They're a never ending cycle, a blender of comparisons. Wanting another girls hair or color of skin.

SECURITY & CONFIDENCE AREN'T LOUD

Security and confidence aren't loud, they don't make noise. No need to make a show that annoys.

I'm not surprised at my total whirlwind overnight success cuz God always said He'd give me this.

God doesn't want us underestimating ourselves--it's an insult when He's put words in our mouths.

It was the stupidest thing I ever did living with you kooks but I learned more than a library of books.

SUCCESS AFTER SEASON OF TREASON

But it was only after a season of duress: backstabbing friends, accusations to ruin, female tyrants.

That season of treason lasted decades and I literally had to outlive the broads/phony feminists.

Paul said be content where you're at and I think I proved it by living in a tiny dusty cabin like that.

There was a time when the queen let a bum in and he took over everything. HA HA can you imagine?

You won't be loved by liberals when the women are mean jezebels and the men are beta males.

ACCUSATION TO RUIN

Living in peopled environments I was always shooting at shadows, overreacting, maladapting, sick.

By the time of retirement you're finally free but then you don't have that long to enjoy it see.

Gossippings, murmerings, backstabbings, whisperings, dyads, jealousy triangles, resource guardings.

Resource guardings: you see this around will reading when sisters secretly collude with attorneys.

INSECURITY AND SHAME

After they sinned Adam and Eve looked for coverings: that's the first sign of man's insecurity.

Sin creates a void on the inside, that brings on insecurity and that shows on the outside.

God did not create us with insecurity. It's an external force or an underlying line of thought see.

Insecurity comes from trauma or training. An event breaks you/they degrade you = insecure see.

Trauma or training: Insecurities are not innate but occured after your birth date and you've paid.

God gave us power, love and a sound mind. Not a spirit of fear, timidity or inlaid insecurity.

THE WORLD TRASHES SELF

The world is constantly misshaping our sense of self so the mind must be renewed to stay well.

A queen conscious woman will always strive to eliminate insecurities, negativities and false identities.

ACCUSATION TO RUIN

She ACTS and postures like a Boss Chick but she hasn't actually realized it, she's just a mean bitch.

Walking around and high falutin is arrogance too. It's so prevalent it's embarrassing and hardly cute.

An insecure woman will ruin the power couple chemistry because kings are not attracted to it see.

The hands of insecurity from previous bad relationships ruin the power couple ambience instantly.

You pray for a king of a man and when he comes along you show your insecurities and he's gone.

ROYAL COUPLE OBSTRUCTIONS

God brings an amazing couple together to conquer the world and you trash it with insecurity girl.

You can't pray for a king but have the insecurities of a girl but this happens all the time for sure.

A high value man of like mind is what the queen seeks. Can two walk together lest they be agreed?

Your insecurities will always demote you from what you're qualified for. Is that you at his door?

Your insecurities always demote you from what you're qualified for. Is that you calling/at his door?

RUIN FROM NO SELF-CONFIDENCE

Your lack of self-confidence will always ruin the power couple chemistry and you'll become a liability.

Without confidence you overestimate others and underestimate yourself, bringing imbalance.

ACCUSATION TO RUIN

Lacking self-confidence you overestimate bums and underestimate your own greatness hon'

Such insecurity draws her to relationships with bums where she feels insecure and inferior to them.

What is it about a bum that you can't live without? Your insecurities have made you a deluded nut.

Please don't misunderstand but addiction to bums is common. Like a magnet as they latch on.

Her insecurities make her so delusional she actually esteems a bum who degrades her too.

He's not a clown cuz they have jobs. This guy's a bum you're into--a clear sign you've lost God.

Saying you can't live without this bum is demonic and you need deliverance from this nonsense.

Insecurities blind you to your greatness then treachery will tear you down despite outward sweetness.

Her insecurities see that bum as irreplaceable, that's how psychology works and it's dangerous.

When the prodigal son came to himself he realized how great he'd had it and how bad it now was.

COMING TO YOUR APEX

It's so exhilaratingly wonderful to reach your epitome--crown of glory--tho' just before the end see.

It was my journey after imputed shame/mental illness from mal-adaptation to people I guess.

I was banned from ED groups by broaching ancillary symptoms like kleptomania/promiscuity.

ACCUSATION TO RUIN

I was banned from ED groups for telling em how to eat for ectomorphy [slim] without symptoms.

They don't wanna talk about those things, they wanna keep it cold and clinical and it's all bull.

Worldly pains squeezed me like a python until out came divine nectar in form of 70,000 proverbs.

I'd never witnessed such a dystopic free speech-hating atmosphere as a girl's ED group, pooh.

These women don't know nothing about nothing they just wanna dominate and impose see.

They would never let em eat once a day in an ED clinic. They have to stuff their face thrice a day, ick.

INTERLOCKING JEALOUSY PATTERNS

Interlocking jealousy patterns are an example of insidious lines in groups acting like chicken coops.

I was happy, creative and free but when I re-entered the family tree I meat horrifying lines of tyranny.

Toxic shame is so uncomfortable it helps to know it's passed on from previous generations long ago.

If when the group comes against her for her sins she just feels more traumatized, she spirals down.

The one good thing is it drew them out. It flushed out all their meanspirited jealousies/being bought.

How did we get into this mess? Because the population acquiesced: trusting despite corruption/graft.

Thru this process political correctness gives way to more insidious forms of groupthink and mob rule.

ACCUSATION TO RUIN

GROUPTHINK AND MOB RULE

Lockdowns are accepted in the name of national security--no matter how extreme or unreasonable.

We stand intimidated by red flag laws, watch lists and zero compliance policies of police states.

These tactics aim to keep us fearful and compliant and it happened when Trump left, in a minute.

I'm not mad at Trump like my compatriots are. I think he's waiting calculatingly to pull his Trump Card.

BUT if enough people refuse to cooperate in their enslavement it can be mitigated and rolled back.

TARGETS GET NERVOUS IN PUBLIC

I grew terrified of my German sisters who were gossipy, calumnious, meanspirted and ruthless.

They accused me of preposterous and evil things, I feared their misjudgment/escaped into drink.

The ruthless intricacies of these sick systems teach us to be extremely careful and humble in a bubble.

Tho' a writer I'm very careful with what I say and mostly I don't say a thing: it's a very dangerous time.

The antisemitic buildup in Germany is how it happens: it starts with putting em down then restrictions.

I was so terrified of my German sister it hurts my stomach to recall it. Inner rage suppressed = psychotic.

The white man is hated now like the Jews in Europe then and I'm afraid another South Africa's coming.

ACCUSATION TO RUIN

German lower class and not-so-smart: give em a little power and they're the WORST of the lot.

How can they deny cultural differences--one can get a Ph.D. in Cultural Anthropology, it's obvious.

You could do anything you wanted to a Jew and get off: take his cow, beat him up in a crowd.

If the cult gets everything it wants in 2021 it's going to be difficult or impossible to become/stay great.

THE NARCISSIST IS SO BORING

The narcissist is SO incredibly boring but to the foolish peanut gallery so adoring, he's the king.

He hurts those closest cuz they're the ones he knows. As he branches out he'll spread the woes.

Knowing you need protection [from him] is the thing dividing you from miserable past to wonderful future.

You were the victim of social tyranny but so were so many others. Broaden your view, get a breather.

You were the victim of sisters or brothers but so were so many others. Get outa yourself for oasis.

He sickeningly puerile and ingrown. But according to him he's the smartest man the world's ever known.

SINNERS LOSE THEIR GUILTY STAIN

Sinners lose all their guilty stain--wasn't that the main song we sang? White as snow and start again.

If he's gonna be a pottymouth like that you don't go on his show. Do you hear me girl? Go HIGH not low.

ACCUSATION TO RUIN

If he's a pottymouth you know God's not in it. The right link for you is decent thru and thru, count on it.

He thought I was flaking out but it was cuz he was a potty mouth and I lost interest fast, the louse.

Homelessness in the Cities: an unbelievably low level of existence unimaginable to most people.

His bad behavior changed the archetype of him completely and I was a little scared at the transmogrify.

When an archetype changes--prince to toad--the reactions are dangerous as revenge takes hold.

SIN BRINGS GHASTLY UGLINESS

He "did" someone and it changed his archetype instantly as respect was lost from all posts accordingly.

Older women, younger men. It could be a good thing or a disaster on her self-esteem. I'd go lightly.

Then he got mad at you for your cold new attitude and then from there it spirals down for the rare.

They think it's them, but it's not them. It's beauty injected by God, who can withdraw it then you're odd.

Think what you want, I don't know you now. The archetype has changed and I feel I never did somehow.

When the archetype changes it's an entirely different person. What changes it? Diet, actions, SIN.

You went so far down I doubt you'll ever get it back, but it scared me to see what you're like in fact.

WHEN HE SWITCHED TO A MADMAN

ACCUSATION TO RUIN

I don't know what you did to switch to a madman but all I know is the love is gone and you did it man.

When that archetype changes, watch out! When it flips from bad to good they're all ashamed: wow.

Your whole demeanor changed overnight. Hey, what was it you did man to bring on this sudden blight?

The archetype we fall into caricatures it's basic properties so we're just a CARTOON of our idiosyncrasies.

With prolonged trauma your self-esteem plunges. That's why you're frozen, can't talk or send messages.

No one understands the traumatized. She's shut down, can't act, seems really unreliable--flaky in fact.

Inside, a groan: One can know and speak psychology while being traumatized by their own.

She committed to something and flaked out. What a terrible person--emotional illness is disallowed.

Oh well, you'll never understand. You've got a mass of fans, go with them. You're too distracted, amen.

HOW TRAUMA BLOCKS SUCCESS

After trauma the body/mind naturally seeks to protect the self from possible harm. Avoidance, alarm.

After trauma he is easily provoked and lacks the stable core of love keeping the average person afloat.

When you've spent much time rebuilding self-esteem after trauma you don't take chances with more drama.

Any failure will cause the "new" self-esteem to crumble so one doesn't take chances/lives in a bubble.

ACCUSATION TO RUIN

Trauma causes IRRATIONAL fear. You can't even risk a slight failure again, please understand dear.

Fear of failure: People with traumatic background can relate to that, it immobilizes you for sure.

Fear of failure is a huge blockage and if you don't have a bed of healthy self-esteem, it's catastrophic.

You give up to avoid going into another painful shame spiral. You avoid trying to eschew hell.

"They threw paper airplanes at me. I went into a tailspin and I was never the same" said the batty lady.

FEAR OF SUCCESS: PATHOLOGICAL ENVY

Fear of success: You minimize self from fear of getting ahead due to pathological ENVY of the walking dead.

Every single achievement, they said I didn't get it. Every single blessing, they said I didn't deserve it.

The envious become obsessed with destroying you for its the only way to regulate themselves too.

Focused: Narcissists have very fragile self-esteem so if they're envious they become mad/obsessed.

When in the spotlight, when I'm interviewed or gain praise my brain says "danger" due to the old days.

View: Dim yourself, shrink yourself—the brain is trying to save you, for if too exposed they'll DESTROY you.

DON'T GIVE EM A CHANCE

By avoiding important life-changing interviews I won't be destroyed. The brain tries to save girls/boys.

ACCUSATION TO RUIN

Standing up to ridicule is essential for warriors but the traumatized cower--must pray for God's power.

The pathologically envious will MALFUNCTION in their rabid desire to destroy for self-regulation.

The envious will do anything to DIMINISH whatever you've accomplished--that alone blocks you success.

Pathological enviers are very dangerous so if traumatized it makes sense why you'd dim your light for us.

A victim of pathological envy can FEEL the jealousy when it happens, a destructive energy that dampens.

There's pathological envy of mothers destroying daughters, even making them into paupers.

In a true nervous breakdown the nervous system is destroyed and one is hospitalized: no fun.

FRENEMY ABUSE

The abuse from frenemies can be so destructive the fear blows all thresholds, emotionally exhausted.

Your enemies aren't around, they aren't hurting you. It's frenemies confusing you from mixed signals.

When you feel hopeless your mind is in a constant negative loop. Back and forth and you're no longer cute.

With frenemy betrayal, abandonment and rejection we feel helpless, worthless, hopeless: we give up.

Since past failures were unexpected we fear it's gonna happen again in major disappointments ahead.

Being in constant fight or flight mode the body is exhausted and can't initiate or be bold.

ACCUSATION TO RUIN

STOP RUNNING YOUR MOUTH

You run your mouth so much I can't think. Go get a counselor if you wanna blather rinkydink.

Interview: I don't wanna give em a chance to ridicule because it triggers memories of gradeschool.

Repeating slogans and narratives is not intellect, it just makes you a parrot and I'm sick of it.

Voted the most likely to succeed in high school, when I saw him decades later he looked like a cartoon fool.

He'd been strong, dignified and unique but when he adapted to society it was a lower archetype.

That dilapidated ugliness is not aging, it's the natural evolution of evil. It's progressive you know.

Sometimes you must outlive your obstructors for victory. It's a span of time you're down then UP, see.

NEVER CHASE A MAN

Such brilliant thoughts and utterances, that's what he thinks. Let him think it, they're not genius.

Women: You must never chase a man. It's goes completely against the grain and that's that.

People go from toad to prince, from prince back to toad. It's eternal: the greatest story ever told.

Don't back into aging constantly looking back at that crap. Look ahead/BLOSSOM: new map.

You call it a "lame excuse" but it's not. It's REAL buddy and it's deep, unmovable, like a boulder of rot.

THE PRICE OF EXPOSURE

ACCUSATION TO RUIN

It's not WISE to be so exposed. I don't want exposure! You seem to seek it, unwisely I think, society's tolls.

Despite their proud demeanor, narcissists are cowards. They BULLY their way over others.

Whenever he feels threatened the narcissist bullies to regain control. He has a short fuse, that's all.

Parents love to spoil their kids, pet-owners their pets, that's how it is--but they still mock women and their cats.

I never wanna go anywhere cuz I'm busy every minute doing what I wanna do and none other.

Yes they wanted to share you with ALL their friends but what they put you thru was disaster, amen.

Since we swam in muddy waters we didn't realize how it seemed to others. Stop/let decency take over.

I told you, they threw paper airplanes at me and I never got over it. Now leave me be and forget it.

ARCHETYPAL PSYCHIATRY RULES

A different archetype was evoked and I freaked out man. When a human debases it can be frightening.

I recall when people were frightened of me due to an archetype I was triggering and the treachery.

You must be careful with the archetype thing cuz their brain will fill in the dots with other things.

You'll be ecstatic when not eclipsed by another. Cuza him in your view you've lost what you're made for.

Losing independence is horrific as you're own map's replaced with another so sickeningly different.

ACCUSATION TO RUIN

THE END IS THE APEX OF LIFE

I'm at the apex of my life/career and you're putting me down for getting older? That's what I mean dear.

You didn't bring your friends to meet me you brought a buncha robbers/petty thieves of little things.

You didn't bring friends to meet me you brought grifters taking anything not nailed down like chairs.

You didn't bring your friends to meet me you brought spies and people opening drawers, making notes.

My home is my protection against disrepute, ignominy, gossip, spies, the elements, chaos, people.

You didn't bring your friends to meet me you brought mockers/advice-giving I never asked for.

I told you before, don't bring your friends. My relationship is to you, not them. I vet everyone.

I can't take the violence in your soul, the short fuse. I feel it every minute and need a vacation or a cruise.

Here's the thing: Being a bit older I can see right thru you, I've been there too. It's embarrassing, pooh.

TO GO GLOBAL, BE CONSERVATIVE

I wouldn't talk about sex so much. The rest of the world doesn't think like us, making it mundane as such.

Much of the world is religious/conservative. They're not gonna go along with your indecent narrative.

So if you wanna go international and be the king of your field you better clean up your act and repent.

ACCUSATION TO RUIN

No off-color jokes, for example, to a religious nation like Poland. Wake up buddy or it'll be over.

Nations with freedom also have freedom to sin and that's why they're a trash bin--not orderly, crisp, clean.

When morality leaves a nation those freedoms become bedlam and the whole world can see it ma'am.

Weak women are hypnotized in their homes by wicked men. Yes, that makes sense: don't let em in!

Your home is where everything is and your bed. Of course wicked men want in there then you're dead.

When I let em in my sweet lovely reality became a hellish wartime bedlam and I was fit to be tied.

We are witnessing self-immolation as it's his sin which does himself in from seeds of compensation.

Thank God I overcame those sudden unexplained feelings of either love or antipathy...it's triple Pisces you see.

Good luck to you, it's just not my thing. Don't pressure me, let's just agree to disagree with joy and singing.

FEMALE TREACHERY

I couldn't believe it. When a female came with her friends they instantly started attacking me in a setup.

And the women! Every single one got their friends against me. To degrade each other's in their DNA.

My greatest revelation in life: My mother/two sisters tore me down publicly and created constant strife.

My aunt exposed every lurid detail of my life to every person she met--all the women did that.

ACCUSATION TO RUIN

The moral: Women make mediocre friendships. They can't keep secrets and they always wanna be on top.

Despite my "great ideas" I've learned to sleep on them before acting. That's patience for VICTORY.

Will your female friend go against a group for you? Or will she switch suddenly with their secret rules?

I met a kindly, helpful Christian church lady who proceeded to tell everyone she met all I told her secretly.

Watch out for evil helpers. These ladies worm their way in that way then evoke hatred from the neighbors.

Very few can really help you. More often than not they're an encumbrance or worse, a Trojan Horse.

They offer to "help" you but then ask too many questions and get too involved in your personal business.

NO COMPETITION WITH GOD

I'm not in competition with you. Let's let destiny show the victor as God puts ONE up and the OTHER down.

Mediocre females self-regulate by destroying superior females who now must make themselves dim.

Michelle felt so inferior she'd bring an army over to bash me then act real innocent--an insight recent.

There is no more fidelity and honor in relationships. They'll go in with your enemy and think nothing of it.

The female genius ends up alone which is her opportunity to rely only on God--so it's like a rare shortcut.

Her friends would attack me and instead of saying GET OUT I'd collapse and not understand/pout.

ACCUSATION TO RUIN

This is a complete theory in 134 books taking a lifetime, not motley advice spouted from a carnal mind.

A true Christian is told to COVER another's sins not broadcast them all over town but that's you sis.

Sign of the times: Mothers having pathological envy of their own daughters blocking them in their prime.

PATHOLOGICAL ENVY: FATHERS/SONS

Sign of the times: Sons having pathological envy of their own father's success and hating them for life.

He never listens to me nor reads my work but keeps my homelife on course and puts stability first.

My husband's a great problem-solver and that's the most important thing, not whether he "listens to me".

Nope, he never listens to me but keeps my home life afloat and that's ALL I care about, thanks a lot.

Nope, he never listens to me but he's stable in personality and that means I'm always happy and free.

Because if I can be protected to be by myself--alone--I'm always happy. To maintain that's a good hubby.

I can't say what it would be like if we adapted in the same house. I have a luxury very rare with spouses.

But in truth I think I would hate it. I don't wanna see his negatives nor him mine, it's not aristocratic.

DEEP THOUGHT PEOPLE

I'm extremely deep in my thoughts and don't wanna be brought up. It's always irritating/really sux.

ACCUSATION TO RUIN

Well I gotta guy who won't bother me because he's into his thoughts too--we've got household rules.

You're beginning to get it. We want full-on aristocrat, not this shit--may as well do things right you twit.

I know life's extremes. I've studied the holocaust, I know what can happen, I'll never be complacent.

A rare opportunity never seen before in history: computers where I can study anything/everything constantly.

We protect each other's solitude and that's the saint couples I've read about--they weren't fools.

In order to have the solitude I need he must protect that way to be. Alone, the world flows in unimpeded.

My first husband was no fence. Jolly Jimmy would let em all in and I had no protection/never had a chance.

BASHED FOR HAVING NO FRIENDS

He would bash me for having "no friends" when I just wanted solitude not human obstructions.

The ONLY way to live happily/thrive productively is to wall out all interruption possibilities and wanna bes.

It used to be the older women were aghast at the brazen sex of youth but now they're just as uncouth.

The best husband keeps the world out. When the dust settled I was left standing there world renowned.

Self-imposed monastery, esoteric sanctuary, pet mansion, library, star observatory, stone garden shortly.

The awful things my sisters and mother said about me repeatedly actually brought me to my destiny.

ACCUSATION TO RUIN

OVERCOMING BAD IDENTITY

They falsely accused me repeatedly and me having Pisces energy fought to overcome this bad identity.

Having overcome Cinderella Syndrome of two older sisters and mother hating me I opened up to eternity.

There's a male vs. a female reality. When neurotic they morph into two destructive personalities.

They're little gremlins out to get you man. They come in scanning the environment and making plans.

Feminists are angry man-hating lesbians. Ann Coulter

I'd never wanna get in a fight with a feminist cuz they'll pull their fists—I've been thru this.

Having "borrowed" the male personality she gets more cruel and callous than ever, truly.

And since female is an intricate thinker fighting with social device you could lose your life.

A creative or genius female who isn't social (no time for loco) is destroyed by Mrs. Social Charm for good.

These are ramifications of a morally degraded society when females take control over thee.

JEZEBEL MOTHERS ARE LOUDMOUTH CRANKS

The Jezebel mothers become loudmouthed cranks addicted to power and many drank.

Because Jezebel is out of grace, she messes up big time and now its your problem.

Men have had centuries to learn how to use power but feminists wanna make people cower.

ACCUSATION TO RUIN

You know she's discussing you with others [disgraced], judging from frowns on their faces.

How she fights socially is most cruel. Suddenly you're deposed, fired or flunk school.

She tells all her friends about you and will even bring their advice--you suffocate in this blight.

JEZEBEL FIGHTS WITH SOCIAL TACTICS

The sad thing is Jezebel social tactics is how your mother and sister kept you down: facts.

The Jezebel will get on the horn with your people, to screw you or get more gossip material.

Jezebel doesn't know to mind her own business nor stay in her lane--she's an OFFICIOUS dame.

The Jezebel is an empty vessel so she wants what you have--clothes, tools, friends, husbands.

Whatever you have via marriage she wants to use--like borrowing from your husband [REFUSE]!

When you see these signs of the Jezebel Spirit, get away, escape, pray and STAY away.

The Jezebel Spirit is divisive--it will ruin your home, marriage, church or coffee klatch.

Remember: Jezebel rules thru GOSSIP and sly slander, always balancing factions around her.

She's always planning and manipulating socially so just go into solitude and enjoy your day.

She is so careless with her own life--trusting everyone--that she wrecks yours, hon'

ACCUSATION TO RUIN

THE ANGRY JEZEBEL SPIRIT

The jealous angry Jezebel is always thinking up ways to get her/lower her status/debase.

If I disagreed with her she'd get on the horn and run me down to EVERYONE, Oh lord!

I could feel what was happening so I'd try to appease her more--but she'd just isolate me more.

Another Jezebel I knew would come over to use me for something, never to see me particularly.

And inevitably the Jezebel wants to bring her friends, her brother, her lover till groupthink takes over.

If you irk her in any way she'll get an army of Johns against you--that's why you're blue!

There are very few dignified ladies left, you know. Even the best of em sometimes go low.

Even old ladies swearing/taking our Lord's name in vain. They're supposed to be exemplars, modelin'

These females can't resist the temptation to go low since that puts them in conformity, so...

Women in their 70's getting boob jobs--are they insane? Denial of reality has made them vain.

FEMINIST ACCUSATIONS, GOSSIP, SLANDER

How feminist sister labeled [accused] me was humiliating before having the tools for victory.

Liberal feminist accusations are horrible and demeaning. Just fighting em is debilitating.

ACCUSATION TO RUIN

And then of course they spread it all around, since gossip and slander is the main weapon.

FEMINISM IS ABOUT POWER

The liberal feminist is all about power so she'll slay her own sister, her reputation or whatever.

There was nothing I could say nor do, she owned the social mazeway and would plant the bad story.

She was social, I was not--so she had the power to ruin my rep and it happened day in, day out.

ALL SHE DID was hang on the horn, setting doubts, planting evil seeds, justifying porn.

She's all for abortion and all that crap. She can't be trusted for a minute, a nasty woman in fact.

Jezebel says gross and callous things and that should be a red flag that she'd do anything.

Whatever comes outa her mouth is learned by rote --she doesn't know what she's talking about.

She has a self-image of "loving" but is cruel and insensitive cuz she's really a callous fool.

Anytime someone's milking an image it's filled with conflict and has no basis, it is empty.

And they're ALL milking an image since that's the whole thing in modern social education.

WHY DON'T FEMINISTS ACT FEMININE?

If they're feminists why don't they act feminine, or cease to ATTACK feminine women?

ACCUSATION TO RUIN

The female intelligence is fantastic and right-brained--why give all that up, for what?

There's nothing more disgusting than a manly woman. Yuk three times, come on...

And these manly females are meaner than ever, copying the personality of the other.

The feminine female has POWER but these jealous manly Jezebels can't accept that, ever.

The younger Jezebel will often flaunt her sexuality in front of the older as if it makes her superior.

Liberals will always accuse you of wrong motives and feminists are the worst, haven't you had it with this curse?

He takes care of the bills and practicals and I take care of the house and delicious meals.

It's such a thrill knowing what HOME is. Ours is adapted to us and runs like a Swiss watch.

A HOME TURNED UPSIDE DOWN

Like Stanley said in Streetcar: "Wasn't we all-ok until she showed up, calling me an ape?"

One Jezebel bought a ranch to Lord it over everyone in the region but lost it due to cheatin'

You've got to draw FIRM, QUICK lines with Jezebel or she'll take you over then down to hell.

Everyone's happy and continues to grow. But when there's enmity, envy or third parties...

Sin brings status-climbing/breeds envy--coveting "greener" pastures, a couple's hostility.

ACCUSATION TO RUIN

Then it's like an arms buildup race and even adultery and disgrace comes into the place.

Who can hurt who most: anything can happen in this ambience. It's the devil and he's a sadist.

I've been there and my world caved in. It happened suddenly because I had allowed in sin.

SIN DEGRADES THE HOME

Get SIN out of your house and be thorough. Let no one in if they justify sin or go so low.

For sin is a dirty spirit who seeks to kill your home since he knows that's where you flourish.

Once that sin-justifier is in your home he will tear it down in subtle ways: watch for mistakes.

And who is this dangerous sin-justifier? The little ol' lady calling herself a Christian yet a gopher.

To be all-loving and forgiving she won't discipline and creatives criminals landing in the bin.

I showed her how they wrecked my house and broke the windows and STILL she refused to know.

MY GOD WHAT IS LOVE

You aren't a loving brother if you tell him it's ok to be gay when you know God's against it, but hey...

The so-called Christian is powerless, makes excuses and minimizes sin. He'll find out, and soon.

They will call you a hater for disciplining your own son or daughter--morals are the main divider.

ACCUSATION TO RUIN

Once in-laws get involved/take sides against discipline you'll know what I mean about the system.

Marriage was the first time I could talk heart to heart and know someone's on my side/will do their part.

When all that INTENSE energy of the saint genius went into sin she was horrible back then.

Easy to get discouraged when bankrupt, husbands starts drinking and putting you down.

Suddenly I lost everything, he started drinking and putting me down and I couldn't handle it.

I couldn't handle it because I didn't have the tools--those took years in the wilderness of fools.

How'd I know people were so foolish and stupid? Don't get involved and watch your step.

FALLEN HUMANITY CREATES MESSES

I had no idea how far humanity had fallen. It's shameful, garish, illogical and mean.

They're out for themselves with arrogant narcism and grabbiness is rewarded as something.

They're nothing they won't do when it comes to self-interest and in your life create messes.

Democrats want our guns: victim disarmament where state has the power like Mao Tse Tung.

You can't do anything--society's falling apart. We need guns for protection against upstarts.

I had liberal feminist sisters so I know what it's like to become suddenly D-listers.

ACCUSATION TO RUIN

MERE DISAGREEMENT BRINGS VIOLENCE

If you disagree with even your own family they'll turn on you. I barely made it out, whew.

How do you expect to defeat evil if you agree with it? Just don't hate. Jesse Lee Peterson

He's a white, male, conservative, Christian man of power and they hate him for it for sure.

I had no idea how far humanity had fallen. It's shameful, garish, illogical and maudlin.

Just by telling the truth they'll say "if you can't learn to talk nice/be civil--goodbye, go away.

Human nature: When it turns on you it turns hard and it's tools are despicable: be on guard!

Social chore is the biggest loss of freedom. I don't want any constraints or social expectations.

If you had rejection in childhood the brain will loop with even the mere suggestion of it.

If there was relational trauma in childhood any break from the present will "leak" into it.

LOVING NONDESCRIPT IDIOTS

It's not the nondescript idiot you're with but the PAST which is causing this mental riot.

This is the notion of incompleted mourning: it always causes problems when it rears up again.

I went thru this too: over-mourning idiots as mate selection is really childhood reduplicated.

ACCUSATION TO RUIN

One was a "professional" and a male feminist and I never met anyone as stupid as he was.

This creepy "professional therapist" was also against guns and I suspect he was bisexual at times.

Tho' having gone to a Christian college he rejected it all to become a hippy not worth a dime.

The highly educated hadn't learned a thing and had many friends just as worthless I think.

NONDESCRIPT MATES ARE OK

Why a mate so nondescript? Well because he was nonthreatening and that was my early script.

The "male feminist" will use his knowledge against you and become a twisted mean sadist.

The male feminist is an empty vessel--not a man at all but a gopher get-along with messers.

When I saw him again he was an empty, pasty ZERO--a boring manipulator and definite WINO.

He marries a wimpy weasel without a thought in her head and that's ok cuz he's now brain dead.

He feels "empathy" for poor women but in truth has no feelings for them other than sexin'

Male feminist has so little class that make him a lecturer and they'll demand money back.

He goes for latest books/theories and if you don't know them you're just plain wrong ya see.

OVER-LASTING GRIEF IS JUST A LEAK

ACCUSATION TO RUIN

Your over-lasting grief over that someone isn't really about him but a depressed past so dim.

They wanted to run me outa town/push my face in the mud but I overcame the Elmer Fudds.

I saw they were nothing but was so weak at first they seemed to be superior, overbearing.

I had been made weak from previous systems so vision was blurred and I called em "Sir".

The media that wants us to look elsewhere has shown its complicity in despicable acts: beware!

The same media pointing fingers at Trump for Russia were covering up for Epstein the worst thug.

When in a fallen state everything that is wrong seems right and hell arrives overnight.

If the horse has been dead for ten years it's time to dismount. Joyce Meyer

"Space" gives us time to take a breath and reflect what we truly want but is seen as a taunt.

America will die if liberals continue to use schools as indoctrination centers.

Keep saying all problems due to sin, then you don't have to blame anyone/it's a higher thing.

Mono-systems living in ghettos is not the same as multicultural integration—just sayin'

A MAGNET TO MAGGOTS

Alone, I was a magnet to maggots not cuza me but the Dunning-Kruger (dumbass) effect.

Good vs. evil is everywhere but an inquiring mind is rare.

ACCUSATION TO RUIN

What they would call fun was **NO FUN** and I hated going and just wanted to stay home.

My whole life is in my **HOME** and in my **HEAD** so why go anywhere? Why get stuck out there.

It's beneath anyone's pride to play the victim card. A real man doesn't act that way, he's a diehard.

When those thoughts come up don't "drop into" the feelings again—actively/routinely turn from.

I think I'm finally getting over her/him/them cuz I'm not allowing feelings to drop into it again.

Everything that happened in California is now deleted from mind as learning trauma.

When preparation was over (to the minute) God (thru Ray) moved me to my reward/their nemesis.

Tho' writing of Systems Theory for my Ph.D., I had to experience it to truly understand it, see?

I experienced it thru the Wife/Child of the Alcoholic Syndrome and a gang invading my home.

I experienced it in a small liberal town where there was no justice just be "nice" to everyone.

Privacy rights have been forgotten--the cops even said about the gang "why don't you want em?"

The right to **NOT** associate is constitutional but not in this social milieu, you're a hater if you do.

ENDLESS EFFECTS OF BAD ASSOCIATIONS

The effects of bad associations are endless and for world success its better to be friendless.

ACCUSATION TO RUIN

Trained to be social she rebels against your hateful reversal and hands you over to your rivals.

Suddenly all her silly friends are giving you advice on your work and you can't say "shut up jerks".

Every time we "drop into" we feel waves of sadness yet we keep doing it when we don't have to.

For 17 years I went into my **SILENT** years in total solitude and I was never, ever happier.

I would take long desert walks and look off to the horizon as I transformed with a new season.

Mental "looping" comes from being over-identified with this story so release it to victory.

Remove yourself from "he said/she said" and you'll get out the lead keeping creativity dead.

She would bring evil gossip against me and entangle me in a hellish mystery entirely unnecessary.

It's just words and interpersonal magnetisms of the moment called "reality" but it's not, really.

I became as stoic as a Chinaman and just looked ahead [adapting to the liberal assemblage].

The liberal feminists were hateful to any female who was different from the party line, oh my.

The women were the worst other than the men going along with them/doing their dirty work.

JEZEBEL USES NICENESS TO KILL YOUR SOUL

it's good to be nice to people but Jezebel uses those social devices to kill your very soul.

ACCUSATION TO RUIN

She imposed on me last time bringing her creepy boyfriend and I never saw her again, amen.

They bring their friends around unvetted like you don't have a choice--that's promiscuous.

They come up with a story which spreads around like truth and no one understands--that's the youth.

SIMPLE ROCK SOLID PRINCIPALS

We want simple rock-solid principals of life not an invented narrative causing this social strife.

I ALWAYS felt imposed on no matter WHO it was cuz the inner reality takes predominance.

All gossip is accusatory. I hated being pegged that way cuz the Jezebels made up a story.

They could never judge me without understanding but how could these hick dummies?

Learning to balance these impossible forces (with dunces) was my Ph.D. in the streets.

It was a land without justice where bad was called the best--can you possibly believe this?!

I lived in a world without justice (where wrong is right/right is wrong) for 17 years 'til I met my soul mate—happy tears!

He explained the difference between liberals and . conservatives, releasing me from my prison.

I saw my whole life with new eyes--like being hung up on creepy guys who want guns seized.

I wanted a real man not a beta male who succumbs to false narratives and then sadism!

ACCUSATION TO RUIN

NICE PEOPLE HURT US MOST

The "nice" people hurt me the most as their plastic image implodes like they saw a ghost.

The "nice" lady's chat only goes smoothly when in a crowd of similarly maladapted phonies.

"Who's superior to who" is the bottom of the social game: status-climbing/controlling thru blame .

It can be very frightening seeing what people are like for the first time, but NOW you can climb.

They're creepy and cruel and don't even know it as they become rude as society's mules.

To maintain status they'll do everything but kill us and even that happens in the megalopolis.

IDENTITY IS RELATIONAL

Identity is relational: They see themselves against the ground of how they see you--as a criminal.

When you change or grow it throws their nervous system into a spin as felt status is falling.

With your sudden recovery/growth it's a SHOCK and they'll do anything to bring you back down.

That's the sick system after sin walked in and thus we must be THOROUGH in repentance.

Now that you know what they're like, be like Mother Theresa, take pity on neurotics so childlike.

Don't get hung up again with them and be careful who you have as friends/VET EM.

ANY INVOLVEMENT DISTORTS REALITY

ACCUSATION TO RUIN

Any involvement distorts reality but those allowing growth bring on total unabashed clarity.

Then it's a warm hand assisting you ahead not a dam liberal feminist boot on the neck.

"Taught to be social" means strict conformity to enormity and its really communist training.

It's not about social niceties of polite society but dogged, brutal human system tragedies.

There's no more decency and even the "nicest" show grossness from videos they see.

They think a slut is "cute" from seeing Blanche in the Golden Girls which made so much loot.

Blanche ruined an entire generation of women who had affairs or left their poor husbands.

Blanche was written as "cuter" than the more normal women who wouldn't sleep with vermin.

Debauched comedy registers subconsciously as a green light even in the nice/noteworthy.

DELETERIOUS DIVERSITY

Why are all the ads now inter-racial? Black and white couplings design to shove down globalism.

I mean ALL the ads. It's been decades since I saw both were white and it's an increasing fad.

Blacks, Hispanics or any ethnic gravitates to their own kind but if whites do it it's mean?

People affinitize together but if whites do its "white nationalism"--a nasty peg for birds of a feather.

ACCUSATION TO RUIN

With each immigrant we are more a minority in our own country, a gift from our ancestry.

And yet silly women or fallen churches continue to bring em in under dubious auspices.

Watch what you speak because people loop, leak, turn up the volume then they REPEAT.

As conflict triggers core beliefs and an echo chamber cries for release there is NO peace.

CAUTION OF PEOPLE IN THEIR SYSTEMS

When it comes to people in their systems with other people you must be VERY careful.

Instead of looking at things with face value it's create a narrative about it and that's the scoop.

The new narrative is divorced from cold facts and is just about gathering evidence of crap.

What additional meaning are you LAYERING on top of the factual experience? Think on this.

You've controlled your friends/environment but with solitude you won't have to, think on that.

Instead of allowing all thoughts, think: "am I looping, leaking, dropping into or is it the truth?

Ask: Am I layering the past onto the present, am I magnifying because it triggered a torrent?

By getting stuck in a narrative I'm feeding I remain in a system that only increases insanity.

You must get out, ignore or avoid it to cut out connections and retrieve your own trip.

ACCUSATION TO RUIN

LAYERING FUELS FALSE NARRATIVES

Since it's layering that fuels the false narrative it triggers panic and therefore deviance.

The circularity is like a rat on a treadmill: You are obsessively looping in a mind never still.

CATCH that thought and analyze it: is this the past, am I layering, looping or distorting the facts?

Therapy lies in understanding the brain. It layers, loops, leaks and repeats it all again.

QUESTIONING PERCEPTION

Questioning perception gives a BREAK in the self-perpetuating circle of mental/emotional havoc.

We're trying to interrupt the obsessive hook of repeating the story/reinforcing suffering.

Learn to know that you matter, despite a feeling state triggered that you DON'T matter.

Recognize thoughts as fallible, susceptible to falsehood from layering as the brain will.

And God said about this: Whatever did or didn't happen miss you can count on Me fixing it.

Whether I matter or don't matter, I'm ok with myself because I belong to Jesus who is my Savior.

The superior female writer arrives to success exhausted but overcoming is always rewarded.

Cure to interrupt obsessive thinking: drop the story.

ACCUSATION TO RUIN

Honey, it's just a story. No matter how disparate the facts you have made it a defeat so gory.

UNPEELING MEMORY HISTORY

Coming outa denial reveals layers: back two years, then ten, then re-experience earliest years.

I finished the 80's then started on the seventies and on my, the horrid embarrassment, please!

It WAS another person in this skin, with Jesus we're all redeemed and made new again.

The thoughts, actions and past-times were of another human being for I am made new again.

Thoughts stream in--let em go. Start loopin'/leakin'/repeatin--deny everything you know.

We do not think thoughts but choose em as they stream by so tell Satan to go away, bye bye.

In other words, take charge of your mind--the characteristic of successful and the refined.

Aren't you hungry living on grapes and smoothies? Ok for a spell but I'm not going that way.

Stop hurting yourself by thinking of those you "lost" but were bad for you/weren't in the cards.

Go on, life is short. Stop compulsing over things you can't do anything about and live to the hilt.

Get kids outa the schools and we'll have Renaissance of liberty, learning and intellectual pursuits.

ALCOHOL ALLERGY IS GENETIC

ACCUSATION TO RUIN

What I went thru learning I could **NEVER** drink even a drop--my genes was why I had to stop.

The hangovers, bad thoughts and **PANIC** were signs of an alcohol allergy which was gigantic.

My ancestors were either famous orators or died in the gutter of this terrible alcohol fetter.

My relatives came to me before they died and told of this strong genetic predisposition, bonafide.

A mere drop or atom of the stuff switches the brain to another system and it's never enough.

Even a little wine, Nyquil or cough medicine is enough to ignite this whirlwind, a blight.

ALCOHOL A CONDUIT TO THE DEVIL

Alcohol is a conduit to the devil and not just for me, many have had their lives ruined tragically.

If you can take it go ahead and enjoy it. But if you can't you'll be successful only free of it.

When drinking all normal inhibitions were lost and I became the worst of the lot, God help us.

The education system goes from bad to worse as they push perversion ending in the hearse.

Not teaching how to read and write but gender confusion and climate change fright.

I guess when you're dealing with genius you tolerate what most would find offensive. Bea Arthur

Stop thinking you miss him cuz you DON'T--it's just a leak in your boat to the childhood below.

ACCUSATION TO RUIN

LEAKING TO EARLY TRAUMA

Leaked to early trauma, Elmer Fudd seems like the handsomest and strongest man on the planet.

It's not him you're sensing but the terror of childhood rejection mislabeled as excitement.

He's nothing like ancestors bigger than life but after falling your mate selection created crisis.

Mate-selection is based on life-level attraction and with self-disgust it can't help but decline.

When the Potter was done and I was finally right, in came the right Christian man for my life.

How do you start? It's wherever you separate the present from the past. Bea Arthur

Remorse over bulimia to console: Think of celebrities with Queen's disease: Dianna, Jackie O.

The Jezebel is a friend from hell.

Whenever they bring up the bad past you must ATTACK BACK cuz it's no longer fact.

I made believe Hoss and Little Joe were my brothers. I felt so happy with my strong family in the frontier.

GREAT AND MARVELOUS WORK AND WONDER

Let this minute separate the future from the past and may you all have a creative life at last.

Creativity comes and goes ya know. You may be a genius when sober but when drunk, laughable.

And then everyone will talk, laugh or be disgusted by it and that's the end of it--your career.

ACCUSATION TO RUIN

So be careful/take nothing for granted for you can be an overnight success but bust just as fast.

Lord, I need you. I can't do anything without you, fill me. I am useless without you, live thru me.

I didn't love them--Tom, Dick or Harry--I just wanted God and mislabeled the whole thing, how odd.

Strangeness: the High Depravity of the Elite.

Whenever a trigger says you don't matter pull out of the story cuz that narrative is the fetter.

STATUS QUO MAINTENANCE

You DO matter but the world conspires to maintain the status quo with you kept down below.

It's a matter of homeostasis to keep you from your oasis cuz their identity depends on this.

Your success, luck, good breaks or looks drives em crazy with envy--that's the human race honey.

Memory reviewing is like an onion unpeeling as you re-see your entire history--so sorry!

It's worse for women growing up in this generation for there's SO much more to face again.

See embarrassment as a spirit and greet it when it rises up--this cog in the wheel disperses it.

SELF-FORGIVE EVENTS OF YOUR FALLEN STATE

In a fallen state anything can happen and anything DID but that was another person back then.

ACCUSATION TO RUIN

Looking for evidence like a detective: so intensely impacted by emotion, brain shuts down.

Anxious Preoccupied Attachment Style means you're tunnel visioned and neurotic as hell.

It's becoming hypersensitive to the frequency and patterns of relating so REAL life is fading.

Love addiction is the most inveterate/all-consuming and it's called codependency.

DECOMPENSATION: THE GREAT FALL

To be left suddenly is to have the life sucked out of you: decompensation, psychic tragedy.

The same trauma tho' could be a psychic OPENING: ask God to help you, He's willing.

You should only want who wants you and he/she may not be what you're looking for too.

Don't forget: attachment injury and grief is a LEAK from the early trauma before you could speak.

You can have the idyllic life you envy in others—it's a mental thing as I proved in a shack in the desert.

God put me in a position where I was so imposed upon I woulda done anything to be alone.

When I finally got solitude my little shack lit up like a castle with 1000 acres on the outside.

I was free everytime I looked out to eternity. I related to great minds from history, a new reality.

PUSHING BOULDER UP A HILL

ACCUSATION TO RUIN

I pushed this boulder up the hill and have an inch more still and then only God can fulfill.

The hyper-alert love addict sees minute patterns "between the lines" and it's a hellish time.

The perception of the wife of the porn addict is even more acute and often ends in suicide too.

It's a hellish state being hungup on a creep whether he's clever or not your life is ROT.

Find someone who's responsible. Does he pay the bills, solve problems, keep things stable?

All that matters to me is he pays the bills and keeps our glorious homelife afloat and fulfilled.

The more intricate the patterns the more hyperalert to minute changes in the members.

GET BORED AND SWITCH

Allow yourself to be bored with the news--you've heard it all before/they're preaching to the choir.

Some great presentations out there but you already know it all so abstain from seeing more.

See life as a PIE--a time budget with limitless opportunities--so don't waste your time!

I got a lot from one then wasted ten videos trying to get more but this wasn't in the cards.

SEE YOUR WORK AS GODLY

See it as godly: the culling of information in pure synchronicity but then switching early.

There are literally billions of videos so stop your foolish consistencies and enjoy utopia.

ACCUSATION TO RUIN

Explore history, psychology, Europe and the refined--but MOST importantly, your own inner mind.

An empty vessel is now filled out to depth and character, a firm foundation preventing hell.

Go inside--the INNER JOURNEY is most fascinating and endless despite being friendless.

Being friendless helps since people are an encumbrance to recognition of the Tremendous.

God said we'd always have one good friend on the journey, my husband was mine/thanks honey.

My work couldn't resume 'til husband was a fence against the dense then it all came out fast.

FIGHTING RESISTANCE BUILT MUSCLE

I was a magnet to maggots as God taught me about borders and then to release old baggage.

I learned to HATE surprises like a knock at the door--any interruption to MY plans were a chore.

Suddenly people were avoided as an encumbrance and life was much easier: I could advance.

I had no idea I was meant to be this way. I was told to be social and put up with the fray.

No one tells the truth in social discourse. It's all about flowing and conforming to the gross.

If my good fortune comes from God for being good, why should I share it with you, an evil hood?

God puts one up as He puts another down, that's how it is. Now that you're jealous I'll just withdraw.

ACCUSATION TO RUIN

SHIT ON SHARING

Why should you share your good fortune--which comes from God--with past scoundrels?

Don't torture yourself with thoughts of the pasts' thin escapes. With God that's always how it is.

The bible says to COVER their sins. Not shout it from the rooftops to anyone who would listen.

Is it relationship PTSD or just learning from your mistakes? A lifetime aversion to snakes.

God puts ONE up while He puts the OTHER down--that's success, not coming from the east or west.

I will never, ever, put myself out there for appraisal, whether from publisher or any other mortal.

DOWNPULLING FAMILIES

A man's worst enemies are in his own house. Imagine the depth of pain--and family is the worst?

Undoubtable facts: family members getting other family members sent to concentration camps.

TREACHERY: Family archetypes like the Cinderella Syndrome are automatically incendiary.

"There's no house big enough for two women": old saying never loses truth as they be envyin'.

Leading female/Mrs. Social Charm will always get a head guy on her team to come against a she.

Now that you see, you see--don't seek nurturance from old posts who threatened/rejected thee.

ACCUSATION TO RUIN

Old toxic memories are there to propel you forward not weigh you down, use them for benefit now.

SINGLE WOMEN STAY HOME

A single woman without protection should just stay home. Self-improve, pray: God brings a man along.

Rather than be alone I went out when single--felt like a pin cushion after that ridicule, people are cruel.

My God saved the queen. In another thin escape from not learning from my mistakes I am free again.

I stay home with my own man or alone with my cats and that is that. The social world is the past.

All these memories vaporize the minute you die. Think of that--it's only this plane keeping em alive.

Give em a chance to judge me, quickly/unflinchingly? Hell no, never again, God'll bring the right man in.

Trauma brings boundary & moral collapse. Think of that--it explains the degeneration of families fast.

The young human witnesses unacceptable horror which shocks a nervous system to split into factions.

Are you ignored or hidden under God's hand? Cuz if that's true you'll suddenly be revealed man.

Studies show people lie most of the time. Not for a reason either, whether in peace or wartime.

The Ninety Ninety Rule: People lie 90% of the time and we all believe them 90% of the time too.

It's easy to confuse a complex person with a defiant one, out of fear of punishment he's dumbed down.

ACCUSATION TO RUIN

POSITIVE DISINTEGRATION

My years in the desert could be called Positive Disintegration before becoming whole again.

I crumbled to nothing then thru unique over-excitability integrated at higher mental levels = stunning!

Level One: biological desires combine with sociocultural markers = no true personality uniqueness.

Critical for unique development is autoeducation and autopsychotherapy: you're self-made see.

Peer pressure constrains uniqueness by a group view externalizing values, morals and conscience.

Creativity is funneled into forms following/supporting the existing social milieu thinking its all ok too.

If a society becomes corrupt, these types--the majority by the way--will not dissent, ok?

UNAWARE SOCIALIZATION

Socialization without self-examination leads to a robotic existence called the "robopath" for instance.

Social justifications used: "Of course I break the speed limit, everyone does": social limits are moved.

Genius moves beyond a socialized view to higher development thru personal disintegrations: whew.

Over-excitability makes genius reactions to disintegration EXPLOSIVE into far, FAR higher realms.

Crises challenge our status quo causing us to review our values--the more intense the higher our ideals

ACCUSATION TO RUIN

A unique value structure results called "positive adjustment"--now you're whole not a nut.

A higher state is perch from which all things are now seen/evaluated, no more socially-dictated.

OVER-EXCITABILITY IS NECESSARY

Their mistreatment propelled my over-excitability, disintegration/self-questioning to VICTORY.

We'll get a majority in 2022 due to treachery but could they not by then have destroyed the country?

I had to go thru all that humiliation to get to disintegration leading to this bliss: highest integration.

If reality is socially/culturally based, then when that goes awry they'll will still agree: e.g. Nazi Germany.

I actually had to go thru two decades of emptiness--ZERO--to reintegrate at my highest levels.

Add to that mix HYPER-EXCITABILITY and you have the proper recipe for a great retired life someday.

Excitability/over-reactivity provides the FUEL for the EXPLOSION as the temporal lobes burst open.

EXPECT DISCORDANCE WITH OTHERS

When I dropped socially-based and developed my own unique take it brought hate: be ready mate.

Be a famous conservative, expect calumny. That's great--who would want that? But its coming

Study the Holocaust, understand the buildup of human hatred--that's the social psych matrix.

ACCUSATION TO RUIN

When you break from a social drumbeat it shakes em all up--it's nonverbal and subconcious much of it.

I came back and was just too different. It was felt on every level and was the end of the rabble.

After stress is resolved the HIGHER unique values reflect a second integration = unique AUTONOMY.

After you went thru all that we saw arrival of the TRUE, UNIQUE, INDIVIDUATED PERSONALITY.

To get this peculiarly unique I had to first disintegrate then over-excite to warm to plate to be first rate.

MISCHANNELED DISINTEGRATION

The over-excitation to disintegration could be like a homeless madman when it is mischanneled.

At this highest level each person develops his own version of what it's like to be a superior person.

History records those who had the most to lose did the least to prevent it happening. Ronald Reagan

We're not clones of God, built in His image means we have peculiar identities though called "odd".

At the highest level exemplars have strong individualistic approaches to problem-solving and creativity.

Advanced development come in threes: overexcitability (OE), specific abilities, drive to autonomy.

OVEREXCITABLE = DEVELOPMENT POTENTIAL

Development potential [DP] comes from overexcitability [OE] from high/increased neuronal sensitivity.

ACCUSATION TO RUIN

The greater the OE the more intense the daily experiences of life. Over-excitability = HIGH.

There are five forms of OE: psychomotor, sensual, imaginational, intellectual and emotional.

Lives of the imaginational/intellectual/emotional OEs are most intense: extreme joy/deepest sorrow.

Steered/driven by their value-rudder [emotional], adding intellect/imagination it's the greatest perception.

With advanced development dynamisms increasingly reflect movement toward autonomy: FREE.

Talents/abilities: People at low levels use em for egocentric goals or climbing social ladders.

At high levels talents/abilities combine with value hierarchy to achieve the unique personality.

SUPERIORITY IS INCREASING AUTONOMY

The drive for autonomy provides fuel for further unique expression and a striving for even more.

This third factor of striving for AUTONOMY describes a motivation to become more one's self daily.

When the spirt of "I gotta be me" takes over it ruins you socially but that's the price for superiority.

Positive Personality Growth comes from Disintegration but only in those with DP Development Potential.

I had the genes/talents/abilities but especially the drive to autonomy from my desert experiences see.

A person with low DP will not undergo disintegration [to grow] even in a conducive environment.

ACCUSATION TO RUIN

Development Potential: high sensitivity **PLUS** a drive to develop differences/autonomy from group.

At the core of autopsychotherapy is awareness that no one can show anyone else the "right" path.

His path led to the Holy Grail but if you take it you'll fail for it is not YOUR path/greatest story to tell.

Overexcitability is a tragic gift for the road will not be smooth or easy: great highs and lows.

STRESS IS THE CATALYST

Great creative potentials bring on a great deal of personal conflict and stress acting as a catalyst.

Tho' stress drives development it comes from the same conflicts both intrapsychic and social.

Conflicts both intrapsychic and social: the baby scratching outa it's shell to find the pearl.

For OC's suicide is a significant risk in the acute phases of this stress: find the self and reacting against.

In the interim isolation experienced by these people may lead to self-harm: learn to be self-gentle.

SOCIAL CREATES HOMESICKNESS

When in social situations I felt a gnawing/aching homesickness--for God and myself I guess.

Christian mysticism is all about privacy and individualism, it goes with capitalism.

The relationship of the individual to God (like Job) not conformity to a religious mob and laws.

ACCUSATION TO RUIN

I don't wanna call it automatic writing but to work with God is so thrilling and I'm willing!

I don't call it automatic writing but I've experienced things that give me an ingrained perspective.

A perspective that turns everything on its head about a bunch of lies we've been fed.

I found my knack: oneliners. Now to make a career of it requires God my Father Boaster.

Writing isn't my "career" it's just what I do whether or not it makes money or a little fame too.

I suddenly realized I flew high above the masses and my years of struggle had built a battleship.

Fighting resistance to social built spiritual muscle and solitude nurtured/strengthened the vessel.

RED FLAG LAWS AND HIX POLITIX

With RED FLAG laws you can expect ANY conduct can be deemed by the authorities as bad.

With red flag laws you can expect your EX to call the feds to come for the guns so be ready.

You know how male and female think the other's crazy so they red flag em to avert a tragedy.

With the second amendment ANY restriction chips away at precious freedoms like self-defense.

Yah people are crazy--all the more reason to keep our guns to defend ourselves and family.

The NeoCons don't want free trade they want the China-advantage so there's your blockage.

ACCUSATION TO RUIN

Texas gov won deportation case: "this was a seditious left-wing insurrection and we stopped it".

Pissed off red states joining together through administrative walls against blundering Biden.

RED STATES ARE REAL STATES

Red states giving protection to citizens who want nothing to do with the grand reset of Obama/Biden.

Always same reversal: Obama types promising the workers then once in switching for globalist perks.

States are manning up and protecting citizens against Biden's incompetence and leftist absurdities.

Unbelievably, since Reagan sound economic policies have actually been replaced by identity politics.

Loving liberals rule over them with indifference to their struggles--hypocrites despite cuddles.

Few presidents have been this cavalier about destroying good jobs but that's what it's all about.

It's been all about destroying the economy from the beginning--leftists want us to suffer/begging.

Freedom of speech and presumption of innocence are hard-won rights taking hundreds of years.

Freedom of speech is the cornerstone of all other freedoms but people vote "haters" away.

LEFT VS. WEST

It isn't left vs. right but left vs. west.

They use mass migration to erode the nation state to construct a globalist superstate.

ACCUSATION TO RUIN

A population replacing itself with unknown others is unheard of in human history.

It is bad to let your culture disintegrate since past generations died to pass it on as great.

Trump's PUBLIC CHARGE rule: no more foreign sponges but Pelosi calls that "racist/bigot".

Swedes et. al. are told they need to get over the fact that Sweden is not their country anymore.

Whites are told to celebrate their own replacement and everyone but their own people.

You can't change demographics of a society without a political, economic and social tragedy.

Chris Cuomo was horrible, he was like an out of control animal. President Donald Trump

RED FLAGS: If you see the truth you're "conspiracy theorist" and will be red-flagged/no good.

DEVIL WORSHIPPERS: ANTIFA

Mexico won't let in LEECHES which would "upset the equilibrium of the national demographics".

The liberal left loves loser immigrants who add nothing and take everything, amen.

The transgender agenda came from nowhere and has metastasized everywhere.

The government schools are brainwashing and perverting children, can't we stop em?

Don't run away from their false narrative but TEACH IT so that then you may counter it.

ACCUSATION TO RUIN

KIDS ARE SMART TO DECONSTRUCT

Kids are smart, so deconstruct the propaganda put out by fake news and they'll accept it.

"Why study WWII depressing crap?" Cuz right before our birth millions were killed and we owe them that.

Is it loneliness or ecstatic cornucopia? It's entirely how you look at it but one is loneliest in a crowd I'll betcha.

The Epstein thing symbolizes awakening with the screen drawn back revealing evil manipulating.

ELITES: They just went in there in the middle of the night and murdered a high-profile prisoner.

WHITE MAN TARGETED LIKE JEWS

The white man is the new Jew: a horrifying buildup against those whose ancestors built America too.

PTSD memory gets worse as you get older as you've become more aware of the great danger.

GIVE UP ON THEIR REACTIONS

Never be anxious for "their" reaction for that gives them credence when most are absolutely nothing.

We're on the TRUMP train: that means constantly attacked but being unconcerned in the main.

They are not Americans, they are globalists. They are the establishment and we are the resistance.

Media darlings: They are there to gaslight people into accepting perverse, destructive things.

ACCUSATION TO RUIN

We see liberal buyer's remorse with Biden. That's what happens with arrested development.

That awful toxic shame that's passed down grows and grows unless we nip it in the bud ya' know.

Every time I allowed those thoughts the body flooded with adrenalin--how inefficient and mind-alterin'.

You're. anxious to contribute, I understand that. But I can never finish my thought so PLEASE SHUT UP.

It's an agenda to infiltrate churches and to apotheosize them into falsehood: ways to salvation, etc.

HEALTH AND HOME

With GERD, let's start with the gut: fruit smoothies then for lunch MISO soup and a little rice or spud.

I think about a cat and she walks up. It's just amazing how we're on a telepathy and they're so darn cute.

When it comes to pets, give older ones signs they're more important than the younger, and don't forget.

Find a spouse, that makes life wonderful and delicious. Every day's a banquet, a holiday of kisses.

I'm amazed at how dense men have become. It used to be they were meticulous about attire/home.

NEW BALANCE: SWEET JUICY/SALTY STARCH

What is the answer to gut issues when we know it all, have tried em all yet still sick as hell?

Just smoothies is one answer to gut issues since it's pre-digested. Cucumber/pineapple/mint is suggested.

ACCUSATION TO RUIN

Gut issues: Smoothies with cucumber (alkalinizer) ad pineapple (auto digestant) with mint.

If you're allergic to everything what can you do but end up on (specific, not all) fruit smoothies/miso soups?

The only other alternative is to end up on beef only--I've heard they all return to normalcy.

RX for a sore gut: Smoothies of cucumber and mango but now no tomato or avocado.

May not want to live on smoothies but it's the difference between pain or being happy.

Cucumber: alkalinizer. Pineapple/mango: autodigestant so I don't have to hurt anymore.

If digestion is gone then help it along and that means pre-digested smoothies all day long.

Just one piece of pizza and I feel a truck in the gut for two days in immuno-reactions, crazed.

Every time I see a tomato, potato or pepper I think of HEARTBURN and a night of pain/horror.

FRUIT SMOOTHIE/MISO SOUP

Cucumber: innocuous. Mango: harmless. Pineapple: a little acidic but it's ok I guess.

Avocado: Can never have it again, latex allergy is hell on the esophagus so I say Adios.

Bananas: latex allergy [burnie] heartburn misery--but the least allergenic food they say.

Have you ever been car or boat-sick when you couldn't escape it? That's MCS.

ACCUSATION TO RUIN

The Superior Diet is REVERSAL DIETING not any one thing. Now I'm on a fruit cleanse--flying.

God answered: constrain all food to blender meals and you won't have these reactions.

It's a matter of TOTAL LOAD and a budget of digestive energy, so blend everything.

Gut issues: It's too much to ask at this point to digest, so blend meals and keep the cellulose.

Suddenly I didn't have to nap after meals, I was energetic all day and inspired too.

NO MORE HUNGER ALL THE TIME

Yes the body can re-adapt to live on FAT but its first love is glucose--SUGAR-- for us workers/athletes.

As a vegan I was hungry all the time but with fruit and starch I feel satisfied, healthy, even sublime.

A bowl of grapes, a pineapple smoothie and I'm still hungry need sslty miso rice or mashed potatoes w/ vegan gravy.

Sweet and juicy alternating with starchy and salty: now there's never wanting more to eat.

Why must it be EITHER this diet or that? Why can't it be reversals which keep us balanced?

Two days healthy smoothies, one day miso fasting and feeling great from the protein--yes really.

My cats love cantaloupe smoothies and dogs have my bacon in the mornings: happy family.

It's Saturday, our movie day. I love old movies and the genius therein not seen since then.

ACCUSATION TO RUIN

There's just something about German blood: T-necks with shorts cuz we're warm on the bottom.

Why is it called the "Queen's Disease"? Think of them all: Princess Diana, Jackie Kennedy.

MUST HAVE AN INTEGRATING PARADIGM

Honey, you're too slow for me. It drags on and on but I'm into pithy: sudden insights for self's liberty.

On and on you go without an integrating paradigm. That's a conversation not a theoretician so sublime.

I could really help you but I doubt we'll ever meet. You're the best you think and I'm just another geek.

On and on you go but I don't have the time. If it's of God it's fascinating, life-changing, enthralling, sublime.

A theoretical matrix or paradigm is not a hit or miss bunch of advice. It's a DIAMOND directing your gaze.

REAL THEORIES HAVE FORMULAE

Every legit theory is a FORMULA: a perfect diamond pulling all contradictions together in a new view.

FORMULA: ALL disease is obstruction, ALL recovery is elimination then ALL success attracts when done.

We attract what we ARE, not what we SAY we are. It's affinitization--we affinitize with like tones.

When healthy-minded we attract and we REPEL. That's the elimination part-- we must to remain whole.

NARCISSISTS ATTRACT THE SICK

The sick minded will RETAIN what they should REPEL: they're actually attracted to the narcissist spell.

ACCUSATION TO RUIN

I eliminated everything/every person--started all over again in a tiny cabin then God gave me a mansion.

It seemed every person I met was invasive and crass: a grabby, assaultive, presumptuous dumbass.

If they weren't losers on the make/grifters on the take what were they doing in my cabin? Hard lessons.

What a dangerous way to live for a young woman. I see this now, cozily cradled in my abode with the lovin'.

I coulda really helped you, the power behind. But you forged ahead doing your own thing so goodbye.

CATS, FATS AND ED GROUPS

My cats are the smartest due to the [EE] Enriched Environment with music/love and routine in it.

Cater to your older cats. They wanna be more close, they need more affection, they cry out.

We bloat up from false concepts. I stayed in the desert 30 years to avoid this undertow/find myself.

I was banned from ED group for recommending daily fasting. This therapy feels so dystopian.

So you don't dare recommend daily fasting, best foods or diets constraining to food groups: pooh.

The Eating Disorder industry shows cancel culture best. A recoveree speaks and they only reject.

The solution to a skinny wrinkled woman is to FAST her till it all runs clear. Bragg found that in '54.

Bulimics are sick in the head. It's a Fatal Mental Disorder, no old age, suddenly they're dead.

ACCUSATION TO RUIN

You might also call it a sin but in ED groups it's treated clinically/matter of factly, not as sin see.

If feeling guilty she's banned so her guilt won't spread. If feeling remorse for the past she's ousted.

Black wealth dropped 30% under Obama. The blatant liberal hypocrisy is so obvious in America.

THE CREATIVE ACT

Forgive yourself for all the things you did when the devil was in control. It was a dam demon after all.

I'm waiting to be discovered. All it takes is ONE person to say: dear Lord this is a discovery, historical.

I put it together like a jigsaw puzzle but it wasn't me, I simply reformed what God had designed see?

The med school chair was offended when I said I was a "vessel" for the Creative Act and that was that.

It started as a bud then one year became a formula then grew from there to an entire industry for ya.

I'm waiting to be discovered. All it takes is ONE person to say: dear Lord this is a discovery, historical.

I put it together like a jigsaw puzzle but it wasn't me, I simply reformed what God had designed see?

The med school chair was offended when I said I was a "vessel" for the Creative Act and that was that.

It started as a bud then one year became a formula then grew from there to an entire industry for ya.

ACCUSATION TO RUIN

I don't know why I was chosen to be the vessel for this Creative Act designed before my birth in fact.

SNOOTY PUBLISHERS

As long as you're reaching out you're not superior. They should be attracted to YOU, en masse sir.

Nothing happens without God's approval so screw publishers, you got the Head Mogul.

This is a new age. We're not dependent on snooty publishers anymore--for anything ask God for.

I will never put it out there for publisher's purview again. It's hell on earth subjected to liberalism.

Even the "conservative" or "Christian" publishers are like that. Everyone lives in a box/novelty is bad.

God said He has plans to prosper me and you. He's got a PLAN man so ignore ALL other worldviews.

What a revelation: The Christian and Conservative publishers suck worse than the liberals.

Liberal pubs hate me for being conservative/conservative pubs for me not being what they expected.

I got the creepiest feeling of snooty from this disparager of my work, that's the last time jerks.

CONSERVATIVE PUBLISHERS REJECT NOVELTY

Publishers are just as snooty though they be Christian or conservative. It's just the way it is.

I just don't give a dam. I got it ALL OUT before I died, that's all that mattered. Really.

ACCUSATION TO RUIN

These books are the only legacy I'm leaving the earth, otherwise no one will even know I was here.

And they helped me enormously--I had to spit it out in total to become whole, that's the only goal.

I read my grandfather's notebook written 100 years ago, it spurred me on more then he'll ever know.

God put this Creative Act in me, I completed it and of course He has the link prepared too see.

Ya don't make money from writing but in other ways to support the writing, natural as a bird singing.

It set me back talking to snooty dismissive publishers but I'm ok and relieved to know: never again sir.

LOSS is the engine that drives personal growth and maturation or its turned inward to destruction.

A Creative Act that took a lifetime was predesigned by God and He has the link too He said.

Discoveries don't TELL them what to think, they TRIGGER in the reader subconscious analogies.

ELDER THOUGHTS

You wanna pay off the mansion, new properties and Jaguar? Then do as I say--write 18 hours a day.

Black sets you off, goes with everything and I like it see but you gotta have some color recurrently.

A daily fastarian is NOT an anorexic so get that outa your silly notions holding girls back.

Esp when older we tend to sink in our swill. You gotta take action, now: juice your vegetables.

ACCUSATION TO RUIN

He bought a juicer and there it sat for months. It's just too easy to not take action but we MUST.

It isn't that one you're meant to fall in love with and marry, it's the next one. Marion Kellock

The older cat gets 60 brushings in the morning that she KNOWS the younger ones don't get see.

Critical Race Theory [CRT] is the trigger of one thing hon': race war and violent bloody revolution.

Self-appointed elites are far more interested in threats to Europe than incursions into the U.S.

They wanna go right to the top without doing the divinely-ordained work it takes with God.

The cows run to me for their carrots and apples. How could I ever eat them? They're my pals.

When God calls me to a week fast there is no hunger and food is of no use and superfluous.

I'm a hypersensitive, I get huge eyebags with meat. Look at me as a canary in a coal mine see.

The uglification is quite evident in protuberances, lines, pasty complexion, lopsided configuration.

Critical Race Theory [CRT] is the trigger of one thing hon': race war and violent bloody revolution.

Self-appointed elites are far more interested in threats to Europe than incursions into the U.S.

OUR NICHE IN LIFE

I finally found my niche in life: to describe about how crazy people are in quips/nursery rhymes.

ACCUSATION TO RUIN

If I didn't have books stating my case I wouldn't have identity cuz I let others take over so easily.

I'm a thinker and a writer. It's all about how I put things together in my head and it's all the inner

Studies show the quietest people have the loudest minds. That why I gotta be alone, bye bye.

Study other theories but leave time for your own mind. Lose respect for the outer, go deep inside.

Music evokes thought and there is none better. I put it on and I'm in another world/a trendsetter.

If you can let your great works shine then the shit takes care of itself. Chef Gordon Ramsay.

I'm not great just a pliable brush in God's hands. I've learned after forcing a fit just to relax.

They wanna go right to the top without doing the divinely-ordained work it takes with God.

100 KAREN KELLOCK BOOKS

AFFINITY OR MISERY
AGELESS CORNUCOPIA
AMERICA AWAKE!
AMERICA'S DAFT ERA
ARTS OF PALEO FASTING
AUTOPHAGY ON CHEATERS
BACKSTABBING NEUROTICS
BETRAYAL TRAUMA
BOOMERS AND BROKENNESS
BOOT ON NECK
CHAMPION GUIDES
COMMIE NUTHOUSE
COMMIES
COMMUNIST SPIRIT
CONTAGION OF MADNESS
CONTAGIOUS MADNESS
CULTURE CLASH BASHED
DAFT LEFT
DAILY FASTARIAN
DAM RATS
DIVERSITY IS CRUELTY
E-RACE WHITE
EVIL FREAKS (Beyond Gross)
THE END OR A BEND?
FEMALE BULLIES AND FEMI-NAZIS
FEMALE CARNALITY
FEMALE DUMB DOWN
FEMALE POWER DRIVE
FEMINISM AND RUIN 1 & 2
FIX FOR MISFITS
FOOLS & TRAMPS
FREEDOM SPEAKING
FRENEMY ENABLER
FRENEMY LIAR
FRENEMY THIEF
FRENEMY TRAITOR
TRENEMY TYRANT
GENIUS IS HELD DOWN
GLOBALISLAM
GOD USES THE FLAWED
HAZE OF THE LATTER DAYS

AUTHOR BIO

Karen Kellock Ph.D.

Ph.D Political Psychology, UCI 1976
Post-Doctoral: UCI Medical School
Department of Psychiatry
Grants NIMH, NIAAA

Ph.D. dissertation "A Systems-Theoretic View of Pathologic Interaction" made an early mark as the "Wife of the Alcoholic Syndrome". Postdoctoral research at UCI Medical, Dept. of Psychiatry on the systems surrounding pathology on NIMH and NIAAA federal grants: *The Contagion of Madness: The Psychology of Neurotic Interaction and Pathological Systems.* Therapy tool Therapeutic Playwriting introduced the play *Mary and Murv: Gruesome Twosomes in the Alcoholic Marriage.* She taught Abnormal Psychology and Pathological Systems Theory at UC and CSU campuses and developed "the Debris Theory of Disease" in five books and website: (www.karenkellock.org): *Champion Guides, Daily Fastarian, Just Skip Dinner, Arts of Paleo Fasting, Ageless Cornucopia. Manual for Superior Men is a* pick-it-up-anywhere book that you can't put down (20,000 Kellockialisms) and ever on your desktop it should be found (or this Ebook for superior wordsearch of new jargon).